Dog Training

A Guide to Your New Best Friend

Justin Crowe

Table of Contents

Introduction

Everyone knows the saying that dogs are man's (or woman's) best friend, and it is a lot less stressful when your best friend is able to understand what you ask of them and responds accordingly. Whether you are interested in basic obedience training or formal expert training, this step by step guide to training your puppy or dog is a great way to start at home and lay a basic foundation for a great relationship between you and your dog in the future. Good training not only means your dog will obey your commands but can also be helpful in keeping your dog safe. Commands like "leave it" can stop your dog from eating something you dropped that could be hazardous to his health, and knowing your dog will obey the "stay" command can keep him from running into a busy street if someone left the gate open.

This book aims not only to help you teach your dog the basic obedience commands but to also display your options for how to constructively use that basic training in the future (dog related sports, working dog programs, etc.). While it is the goal and purpose of this book to give you a step by step guide to begin a basic training program at home with your dog, we go beyond that to ensure that you have the information necessary to solve most common problems when adopting a new best friend. A few examples of the extra information provided in this book to help you are, Chapter 5: Beyond the Basics (things you can do after you have completed basic training commands with your dog to further your relationship and skill set), Chapter 6: Common Behavioral Problems (because training your dog how to "sit" will seem irrelevant if you spend the rest of your time dealing with undesirable behavior from them), and Chapter 7: Socializing Your Dog (to help you socialize your dog and relieve any worry about them every showing any aggression when introduced to other friendly dogs in a new environment).

In order to help you make the most of training your dog (and to also try to make training as problem-free as possible), we will also include references to several websites that will be good resources to you in the future (should you decide to explore more than just very basic training with your best friend). Two organizations referenced in this book more than once are the American Kennel Club and Therapy Dogs International. Both previously mentioned organizations are good resources for additional information on training, classes, and volunteer work for both you and your new best friend to participate in.

A few tips to make training easier before we get started.

* Remember to stay positive. Your puppy or dog can pick up on negative energy and it may result in them becoming easily frustrated or discouraged during training, thus delaying progress.

* Choose treats that are high motivators. Your dog may easily get bored being rewarded with biscuits or even soft store-bought treats. For training purposes, you may be able to hold your dog's attention better by using a small piece of cheese or chicken breast. It is also important to consider not using the same treat too often. Your dog may start out by loving the small pieces of cheese you offer but this can become boring after some time. Try to alternate which food treats you use as training motivators every few training sessions to ensure your dog will remain focused on you and willing to learn what you are trying to teach him.

* Always reward your dog coming over to you for attention, even if you didn't call them to come to you beforehand. Your dog needs to associate you with positive feelings of praise, so even if your dog was being bad before you called him, praise him for coming to you. If your dog begins to associate coming to you with being punished, he will begin to ignore you calling for him (whether it's to come to you or just to get his attention for another command).

* When training, especially at the beginning, try to stick to single word commands. They are easier for your dog to remember, to differentiate between commands, and will be harder for him to confuse. Longer commands like "sit down" and "lie down" that share a common word can easily be confused with one another. Stick to single word commands like "sit", "shake" rather than "give me paw" and "down" rather than "lie down".

The four training tips given above should get you off to a good start as you begin teaching your dog or puppy the basic commands sit, shake, and lie down. One final tip to get you started goes back to you remaining positive during training, always end training sessions on a good note! Whether your training session for the day was five minutes or an hour, always leave your dog feeling praised and encouraged so that he will look forward to your next training period.

Chapter 1: The Importance of Training

Health & Happiness

Dogs, like humans and cats, have higher levels of serotonin in their gastrointestinal tracts than in their brains. It is important that your puppy or dog is receiving a balanced diet because disrupting the delicate balance of serotonin in the gastrointestinal tract can greatly affect your dog's moods and behavior, thus disrupting your attempts of training. Canine dementia can be caused by your puppy or dog being exposed to heavy metals and/or toxins in processed foods. Be sure you are choosing a healthy, well-balanced food for your dog so that he is not only healthy but happy and able to give you his full attention during your training sessions. It is important for your dog to remain healthy in order for him to, in turn, be happy and more receptive during your training sessions with him. When you feel sick, you often do not want to do work and the same goes for your dog, so start at the very beginning by feeding your new best friend a healthy, well-balanced diet. For more information on what type of food would be best for your dog (based on their breed, age, and lifestyle) please consult your dog's veterinarian.

Making Time for Training

Once you decide to start training your dog, even if you are just teaching a few very basic commands, you need to make your dog's training a priority and stick with it. Make sure to set aside time each day, even just 10-15 minutes on a busy day can be enough to refresh your dog's memory on the tricks you have already taught him. Another common problem with dog training is when the dog is hyper or doesn't understand what is being asked and the owner gets discouraged. Do not give up! Make sure you don't only set some time aside to work with your dog each day but be sure to go into each training session (no matter how brief) with a positive attitude!

You don't have to set aside a block of time to train your dog each day, you can practice your training during the everyday tasks you would do with your dog anyway. For example, when you feed your dog in the morning (or evening) ask your dog to "sit" and "stay" while you fill their food bowl. This will be good practice for following two commands while simultaneously teaching your puppy or dog to be patient where food is concerned. Another way to practice training each day is before you take your dog outside, whether it's to go for a walk or just out in the yard, ask your dog to "sit" or even lie "down" while you put their leash on. You can teach your dog not to run out the door each time it opens by asking him to "sit" and "stay", then opening the door slowly while asking them to hold the "stay" command before you go for your walks. Even these basic commands can make daily tasks with your dog a lot more pleasant for both you and your puppy!

Beyond the Basics: What Next?

Chapter 3 of this book will go into detail about each of the topics being briefly summarized here. After you teach your dog some basic commands at home and you take time to work through any behavioral issues he or she may have, you might wonder "What's next?" Training for your dog doesn't have to come to a standstill after you lay the foundation for training, as there are several programs and activities that both you and your dog can participate in to keep your skills sharp as well as continuing to strengthen your bond.

- Activities and events can be a great way for you and your dog to bond while practicing the commands that you practiced so much in your training at home. There are a number of dog sports such as agility, Frisbee, and dock diving. These sports offer a great way for your dog to get out of the house and relieve some energy in a safe and constructive way that will be fun for you to take part as well. You do not have to be interested in competing in organized events for these sports with your dog in order to enjoy them, you can still practice them and enjoy them as an outlet at home in your own yard. The important thing with canine sports is to have fun with your dog, whether you are in a competition setting or not!

- If you are someone who enjoys volunteer work, you may be interested in having your dog registered as a therapy dog. Therapy dogs require basic training to become certified, in order to ensure that they are compatible with the position. Therapy dogs need not only to listen very well to their handlers, but it is encouraged that your dog has a general laid back demeanor as the environments they visit (nursing home, hospitals, etc.) often require that they be calm and collected so as not to cause any harm or damage to the patients they are there to comfort. Participating in a registered therapy dog program would be a great way for both you and your dog to get out of the house, spend time together, and meet new people, all while brightening others' days. If this is something that interests you, we will go into more detail about how to get started with a registered therapy dog program in Chapter 3.

- You may also be interested in the Canine Good Citizen or S.T.A.R. Puppy Program. The Canine Good Citizen program is a certification offered by the American Kennel Club (AKC) that sets the standard for desirable dog behavior. The Canine Good Citizen certification is a ten-step test that encourages responsible ownership of well-behaved dogs. The AKC S.T.A.R. Puppy Program is a precursor to the American Kennel Club's Canine Good Citizen Program. The S.T.A.R. program stands for Socialization, Training, Activity, and Responsible ownership. This program encourages owners to get their puppies off to a good start through responsible ownership and basic training. Both of these training programs offer a good way for you and your dog to spend some time together outside of your home, while also allowing you both to socialize by meeting new people and new dogs. Furthering your training can only benefit you and your dog in the future, so if these training programs interest you, we will elaborate on how to get started in Chapter 3.

Chapter 2: Start with the Basics (Sit, Shake, Lie Down, Come, Stay, and Leave It)

Let's start with the basics. Three of the most common and basic commands in dog training are teaching your dog how to sit, shake, and lie down at your request. Beyond the three basic obedience commands sit, shake, and down; you can also benefit from teaching your dog to come when called, stay when asked, and to leave it when they are approaching something not for them.

Teaching Sit

(1) To begin teaching the sit command, it is important for you to start off closer to your dog's level. If you have a larger/older dog, remaining standing may be fine. However, if you have a small dog or a young puppy, it may be more beneficial for you to kneel on the floor or be seated in a chair near your dog.

(2) Present the treat of choice to your dog, close to their nose. Slowly move your hand upward from your dog's nose and firmly state the "sit" command. As your dog's head follows your hand's upward movement, his butt should lower to the floor.

(3) As soon as your dog's butt makes contact with the floor, reward him with the previously presented treat.

Repeat these steps multiple times throughout the day to teach your dog to sit on command, and you can eventually reward him with praise rather than food for his good behavior!

Teaching Shake

(1) After your dog has effectively learned the "sit" command, start by asking your dog to sit.

(2) After your dog has held the "sit" command for several seconds, firmly state the "shake" command.

(3) After stating the command "shake", gently pick up one of your dog's front paws and lightly shake it for a few seconds.

(4) Release your dog's paw and reward him with the treat quickly so that he associates the verbal command "shake" with the action of his paw making contact with your hand.

Repeat these steps several times daily until your dog is able to follow the command immediately. After your dog knows the "shake" command and responds quickly, you can begin alternating which paw you are asking for. Or state "other paw" after he gives you the first paw to encourage him to follow the command using both of his front paws.

Teaching Lie Down

(1) Begin by asking your dog to obey the "sit" command. (When first learning to lie down, it is easier for dogs to assume the desired position from a sitting position. You can practice getting your dog to lie down on command from a standing position once he has gotten the hang of the command from a sitting position)

(2) Holding a food reward in your hand, present the treat near your dog's nose.

(3) With your dog seated and focused on the treat in hand, firmly state the verbal command "down" and move your hand with the reward downward to the floor between your seated dog's front paws.

(4) Your dog will now do one of two things:

> A) If your dog lies down right away on the first attempt, reward him with the food treat and praise him for the good behavior!

> B) If your dog doesn't immediately lie down, keep the treat covered by your hand on the floor and be patient. Your dog should figure out what you want within a few moments and lie down for you, and can then be rewarded with the treat.

Repeat the above steps several times each day until your dog is able to respond quickly to the "down" command from a seated position. Once this is achieved, you can then ask your puppy or dog to lie down while they are in a standing position and reward them for mastering this task next.

Teaching Come

(1) To begin teaching your dog or puppy the "come" command, start by putting your dog's collar and leash on them. Next, sit on the floor so you are at your dog's level rather than standing over them.

(2) Give the leash a gentle tug to encourage your dog to move towards you, and firmly state the command "come".

(3) Once your dog takes a step or two towards you, praise your dog and give them the food reward as a bonus.

(4) After your dog begins to respond correctly to the given command "come" with the collar and leash on, you can remove them and practice this in your home free of distractions and then again outside in your yard. This command will be very helpful in keeping your dog out of trouble should you drop the leash while walking or if your front door is accidentally left open.

Repeat these steps until you are confident that your dog responds to hearing his name and the "come" command, even when presented with distractions like other dogs or people.

Teaching Stay

(1) To teach your dog to stay after a given command (or even just while standing), first gain your dog's focused attention by showing a food reward in your hand.

(2) Next, firmly ask your dog for either the "sit" or "down" position. After your dog has responded correctly to the given command and has held the position for 5 seconds, reward them with the treat.

(3) Ask your dog for either the "sit" or "down" position again, and give the verbal command "stay" while simultaneously holding your open hand in a "stop" position toward your dog.

(4) If your dog gets up from the "sit" or "down" position while you are waiting for them to respond to "stay", repeat step 3 again until they hold the position for 5 seconds. Once they do respond correctly to and hold the "stay" command, reward your puppy or dog with a treat and praise their good behavior!

Repeat the steps for teaching "stay" until your dog learns the basics of what behavior is expected when given the command. Once they follow the command, make it a little harder by putting more space between you and your dog before giving the command or by waiting for more time to pass before they are rewarded with the food reward. You can make this command more difficult again by eventually commanding your dog to "stay" and then walking a few steps away before giving your dog or puppy the food reward for good behavior.

Teaching Leave It

(1) To begin teaching the "leave it" command, firmly ask your dog to obey the "down" command. Once your dog lies down, sit on the floor in front of them.

(2) Gain your puppy or dog's focused attention by presenting a food reward in your hand while they are laying on the floor opposite you.

(3) Set the treat on the floor away from your dog (closer to you) and firmly state the verbal command "leave it". If your dog tries to take the treat, pick it up or cover it with your hand and firmly say NO, then try again.

(4) After your dog has patiently left the treat on the floor for 3 seconds, give them verbal praise and give them the treat. You can then repeat practicing this command, adding a little more time each time you do it before your puppy or dog is rewarded with the treat.

This command is useful if your dog should get into something that could be hazardous for them to eat, or on a walk if they look ready to chase a cat or squirrel. The command "leave it" isn't just for treats on the floor as it teaches the general behavior of

Justin Crowe

focusing their attention solely on you when they hear this command, which is useful in a number of given scenarios.

Chapter 3: Leash Training Your Dog

Taking your dog for a walk is a great way for both you and your dog to enjoy being outside while simultaneously getting some exercise. In order to make walking your puppy or dog an enjoyable experience rather than frustrating, it is important that you train your puppy how to properly behave when walking on a leash. Going for walks is not the only time that leash training is important though, your dog will also be expected to behave when walking on a leash should you need to take him to a park, a store, or the veterinarian's office. It is easier to train a puppy to walk correctly on a leash than an older dog, as they have not yet formed any bad habits, so start training as soon as you can to ensure you run into less problems down the road.

- To train your puppy to walk properly on a leash, they first need to be used to wearing a collar (or harness) and leash. Especially with young puppies who are new to "being dressed", allow your dog to wear the collar (or harness) and leash and just roam around the house. It is important that they feel comfortable with these on before you begin training to walk on a leash outside your home.

- After your puppy is used to wearing his collar (or harness) and leash, practice inside. Starting in a quiet, familiar environment (indoors) is important for training because this will give your dog the chance to see what you are asking him to do before you ask him to do it somewhere exciting. It is much easier for your puppy to focus on you and learn new things in a place free of distractions, you can test his skills by taking it outside later.

- While practicing inside, do not worry too much about your puppy walking "properly" with you. It is more important at this point that your puppy is comfortable wearing his new gear and that he understands he is expected to follow you.

- With your puppy comfortable in his gear and willing to follow you around your home while wearing it, it is now time to take him outside to practice walking. Be sure to keep your eyes and full attention at all times, especially in the beginning because he is still new to training. If at any time during your walk your puppy becomes too excited about something and looks as though he may run towards it (and he will because he's a puppy and there's a whole new world out there), get his attention before he acts on the distraction by calling his name or clicking. Once he returns his attention to you over the distraction, reward him with praise and/or a treat. This will teach your puppy that he needs to remain calm and focused when walking with you, instead of darting after everything that interests him (which will turn into pulling you around as he grows).

- If your puppy is eager to give his attention to everything except you on your walks and starts pulling, just stop walking. Your puppy should learn that if he rushes ahead of you or tries to pull you, you will become stationary and he will lose the chance to investigate anything. This will encourage your puppy to calmly walk with you so that he is not interrupted in his investigation of your neighborhood because he will have learned that his fun stops when he begins to act negatively on a leash.

- Keep taking your puppy for walks and practicing the training tips so he learns good manners.

Chapter 4: House and Crate Training

One of the biggest challenges after adopting a new puppy is teaching them when and where it is okay to relieve themselves. It is important to start housetraining your puppy as soon as you bring them home. If you have a crate, you will also need to teach your puppy when he is expected to be in the crate, how he should behave in his crate, and that the crate is a positive environment.

House Training

Tips for teaching your new puppy when and where it is okay to use the bathroom:

- Remember to take your puppy out regularly! Puppies have small bladders, so they need the chance to relieve themselves often in order to prevent them from having accidents on your kitchen floor or living room area rug. Take your puppy out first thing in the morning, and then again every thirty to sixty minutes throughout the day.

- Show your puppy what area of your yard is to be used for relieving himself, and take him to the same spot each time he needs to do his business. The repetition of always relieving himself in the same spot outside will make it easier for your puppy to remember that his favorite spot to do his business is not next to your bed.

- Be patient. Most dog training professionals do not recommend formally beginning housetraining for your new puppy until they have reached twelve to fourteen weeks old. This is because your puppy may not have enough control of his bladder at eight weeks to be successful at housetraining, but will begin to have greater bladder control by twelve weeks of age.

- Do not give up! It may seem like your puppy is having trouble getting the hang of things, but don't be discouraged! Your puppy will have both good days and bad days with house training, and may even go back and forth several times before he really gets it. Just consider that while it only takes eight to ten weeks for some puppies to be housebroken, some puppies take a full year to really be housetrained. Whether your puppy is a fast learner or needs a little more practice, keep encouraging his good behavior and don't give up!

A great tool to help you achieve your house training goals is a dog crate, as this creates a finite space for your dog to spend his alone time and will discourage your dog from having accidents as dog's instinct do not like to relieve themselves in their dens. We will discuss tips on crate training next, however, if you are unable to obtain a crate for your dog you can also try purchasing disposable puppy pads. Puppy pads teach your puppy that there is a space that they can relieve themselves if they feel they must inside while still discouraging them from doing so on your floor. Keep the puppy pads placed near the door you exit to go outside for potty training so they still associate the act with the same general area. Puppy pads can also be a great tool for safety when you have to leave the house for longer periods and know your puppy will have an accident.

Crate Training

Having a fully crate trained dog can benefit any puppy and dog owner. If your dog is crate trained, this will give him his own safe and private space to sleep or spend with his toys. It is also very beneficial to owners as crating will allow you peace of mind when you leave home that your dog is not having too much fun unsupervised at home (and possibly causing destruction). Before crate training your dog, you must first understand that your dog's crate needs to be seen as a positive and safe environment in his mind. Your puppy's crate should be somewhere that he sleeps when you need to have company over, clean your house, or have to leave the home for a few hours. The crate should not be used as a punishment as this will consequently teach your dog that the crate is negative and he will be unwilling to return to it when needed (using the crate as punishment for your dog may also teach him to fear it).

If you plan on having a rule that your puppy or dog is not allowed on the furniture in your home, crate training may also begin to benefit you the same day that you bring home your new puppy. If you allow your puppy to sleep in bed with you when you first bring them home, this could easily become a habitual thing that will be more difficult to discourage as your dog grows. If you do not want to share your bed, put your puppy in his crate the same day you bring him home. Make sure your dog's crate has a bed or blankets and some toys (something he is encouraged to chew on) so that he will be comfortable and not become bored. After your puppy has been separated from the rest of the litter and comes home with you, he may cry or whine a lot the first night alone in his crate. Try putting some of your worn clothing in the crate with your puppy (a shirt that you do not particularly care about) so that your puppy can pick up your scent and feel safe sleeping alone in his crate.

Crate training your dog or new puppy definitely has its benefits, but how do you actually go about crate training a dog?

- When you introduce your dog or new puppy to his crate, make sure it is a positive experience. Use his favorite toys or treats to make the crate seem like a comfortable place for him. Encourage your dog to step into the crate using treats but do not force your dog in as he may become scared or anxious and be unwilling to go in on his own in the future.

- A good way to get your dog to accept the crate in a positive way is to feed him while he is crated. After you have your dog's food ready, ask him to go into his crate. Once he is in his crate, give him his food and shut the crate's door until he has finished eating. After your puppy or dog finishes his meal, let him out and praise him for his good behavior. This will help him associate being in his crate with food and praise.

- Start crate training by crating your dog for ten-minute period, then gradually increase this time to a period of an hour while you are home. After your dog is comfortable and calm being crated for a longer period, you can try crating your dog and then leaving your home.

Chapter 5: Beyond the Basics

Sports and Events For You and Your Dog

There are a number of dog related sporting events that can not only help strengthen the bond between you and your dog, but they also provide good practice for your training fundamentals. These events provide a way for your puppy or dog to release energy and enjoy themselves without resorting to destructive behaviors at home. Some of the more common dog sporting events are canine agility, disc or Frisbee, dock jumping, flyball, and obedience.

- *Canine Agility*: Agility is a sport in which teams of a single dog and handler compete against other teams through an obstacle course. Agility dogs navigate the obstacle course made up of tunnels, weave poles, narrow walkways, and jumps. Training is essential in this sport as the handler must direct their dog to each obstacle in the correct order, and the dog must respond quickly as the events are timed. Agility provides a great source of physical and mental stimulation for your dog. Any dog can compete in agility, and if this sport is something you would be interested in trying you can watch videos of agility competitions before setting up your own agility course to try out at home!

- *Disc or Frisbee:* Frisbee or disc competitions take the traditional game of fetch and turn it into a sport, often with music and tricks thrown into the mix! In disc competitions, teams consisting of a single dog and their handler/owner compete against other teams based on a point system. Handlers or owners throw flying discs far across a field that has been divided into zones, and each zone of the playing field has a corresponding number of points (points increase with distance from the handler). After the handler throws the flying disc, the dog then runs and catches the disc. Disc competitions also feature freestyle disc competitions, where handlers focus more on the tricks their dogs can perform while catching the discs thrown at shorter distances rather than throwing for distance while the dog "fetches" the disc. This sport is another great source of exercise for your dog and will help with your training at home as the sport requires your dog to practice focusing on you while reading your body language. This is an easy event to practice for at home because the only equipment required is a flying disc.

- *Dock Jumping:* Dock jumping (sometimes referred to as dock diving) is an event where the team consisting of a dog and handler stand on a dock, and the owner of the dog throws a toy to a good distance to get the dog to leap from the dock into the water to retrieve the toy. The object is to get the dog to jump as far from the dock as possible. The teams compete to see which team's dog jumps the farthest from the dock into the water (with the distance being measured where the base of the dog's tail first makes contact with the water). Dock jumping isn't always about distance, there is also a variation of the event where the object is height rather than distance. A toy is hung at a height predetermined by event judges, and the multiple teams' dogs jump high off the dock to reach it. The toy is then raised as the dog's succeed to increasing heights to reach the toy until one team of dog and handler is left standing. This event requires your dog to trust you and also provides a fun way from them to cool off while being rewarded with their favorite toy.

- *Flyball:* The previously mentioned sports all involve teams of a single dog and a single handler. Flyball, however, is a type of relay race consisting of teams of four dogs and four handlers. One at a time, a dog from each team sprints down a straight stretch while jumping small jumps along the way. At the end of the stretch, the dogs encounter a "flyball box" (a box with a panel on the bottom that the dogs step on to trigger the box to then release a tennis ball). The dog from each team retrieves the tennis ball from the flyball box and runs back up the course, over the hurdles, to their owner. The next dog on the team then repeats the course, retrieves the tennis ball, and returns to the handlers. This process is repeated two more times until all four dogs have completed the course and retrieved the tennis balls. The fastest team to have all four dogs retrieve the tennis balls and return to their handlers wins the event. This sport allows your dog to not only spend time with you and release energy in a fun way, but it also allows them to socialize with other dogs while you can meet fellow dog lovers. You can start training your dog for flyball easily at home by getting them used to chasing a tennis ball and helping them become comfortable jumping small hurdles in your yard. Once you are ready you can contact a local flyball group in your area to help you train for events.

-Obedience: Obedience is not a sport that helps your dog burn a ton of energy, but it will continue to strengthen the bond you have with your dog while constantly practicing both basic and more challenging obedience commands. This sport requires a single dog and single handler team to perform a series of specified exercises. This is a great way to bond with your dog and continue to push yourself and your dog to work well with each other while performing various training commands. The best part of this sport is that, unlike the previously mentioned sports, it requires no equipment (other than a few treats to encourage your dog to focus on you and your commands). You can easily practice all the required exercises in the privacy of your home, then outside in your yard, and once your dog is responding well to you in private settings you can practice commands in more public places like parks. Rally obedience events are generally open to all breeds, so once you feel that your dog is responding well you can find local obedience competitions to try out with your best friend!

Canine Good Citizen

The Canine Good Citizen program is a great goal for you and your dog to work towards together. With some dedication and practice, your dog can take the ten step test to earn the Canine Good Citizen title (your dog will even carry the letters CGC after their name showing their accomplishment!). The Canine Good Citizen program is run by the American Kennel Club (AKC) and was started in 1989. For many of the program's participants, the Canine Good Citizen certification is the first step toward a larger goal such as participating in a program that welcomes therapy dogs to visit those who are under care in hospitals or nursing homes. Any dog can participate in the Canine Good Citizen program: from purebreds to mixes, all dogs are welcome to show their training and good manners. For more information on how to train your dog and test for the Canine Good Citizen title, you can visit the "About" page on the American Kennel Club's official website at http://www.akc.org/dog-owners/training/canine-good-citizen/.

Your Puppy Is A S.T.A.R.

Another training program offered by the American Kennel Club is the S.T.A.R puppy program. The S.T.A.R program name stands for Socialization, Training, Activity, and Responsibility: four key points in the program's training goals. The S.T.A.R program is a training program offered for puppies of any breed (purebred or mixed) so long as they are under a year old. Puppies enrolled in the program, participate in a six-week basic training course, and must pass a test at the end of the course. Upon passing the program's test, your puppy receives a medal and a certificate to show his or her accomplishment! Many of the puppy owners who participate and pass the S.T.A.R program go on to also complete the Canine Good Citizen certification offered for older dogs. The American Kennel Club's goal with the S.T.A.R puppy training program is to encourage puppy owners to be responsible pet owners while offering them advice on puppy raising problems (such as chewing, jumping, and housetraining) and giving the puppies themselves a chance to socialize with other dogs. If you have a puppy under a year old and want a basic training program that will get you both off to a good start, you can find more info on training and registration on the American Kennel Club's official website at http://www.akc.org/dog-owners/training/akc-star-puppy/.

Helping Others

Whether you have completed a basic training program with a professional dog trainer or have taken the initiative to do all the training on your own at home, once your dog proves to know basic commands you can use your skills to help others by registering your dog as a licensed therapy dog. Therapy dogs and handlers visit hospitals and nursing homes to comfort those who are sick or injured. There are really only 3 requirements for therapy dogs: that they are healthy (and that this can be verified by a licensed veterinarian), that they have a sweet and even temperament, and that they be older than a year (this gives you time to complete basic puppy training that will help in your volunteer work with your puppy or dog).

Any dog is eligible to be trained and become certified as a working therapy dog, regardless of age or breed. If you are interested in volunteering with your dog as a team in making others feel better, you can find more information on how to do so by visiting the website of Therapy Dogs International at http://www.tdi-dog.org/About.aspx. This organization (Therapy Dogs International) was founded in 1976 and they had 24,750 registered therapy dog/handler teams registered in 2012. Therapy Dogs International is a non-profit organization that works to train and prepares both eligible dogs and handlers for their volunteer work as a registered therapy dog team. It is important that if you are interested in becoming a therapy dog team, your dog has at least basic training (sit, down, stay, and come) and is able to remain calm/friendly when introduced to new people/environment.

Chapter 6: Common Behavioral Problems

Like everything else in training, consistency is key in correcting bad habits. If you allow your dog to jump on you or strangers, or chase squirrels, even occasionally they will expect to be allowed to take part in these bad habits regularly. It is very important that you remain consistent in correcting negative behavior; this means correcting them every single time they jump up on a person and correcting them every time they chase after another animal outside. If you only occasionally correct your puppy's bad behavior, they will not know what is expected of them and will continuously act poorly.

Jumping

Jumping is a common behavioral problem with many dogs, especially in young puppies who have an abundance of energy. Your puppy may not seem like a problem while he is young and small, however, this habit can quickly become annoying and even dangerous (if your puppy is a larger breed that will eventually weigh a significant amount) if not immediately corrected. It is important to consider that the longer you allow your puppy to perform this behavior without correction, the harder it will be to break the habit.

Breaking your dog or puppy of their jumping habit should be pretty easy to do after you have already taught him or her how to "sit" on command. Anytime you (or anyone else) come in and your dog jumps up, immediately command them to "sit". You can give the sit command as soon as you open the door, even before your dog actually jumps on you. As soon as your dog's feet return to the floor and the "sit" command is obeyed, be sure to praise your dog for their good behavior. Eventually, this will teach your dog that when they are excited to see you and want to greet you they will receive the attention they desire by remaining calm and collected. Start by asking your dog to sit any time you return from somewhere, and once your dog or puppy is able to calmly greet you, you can then ask friends and family to help your dog practice the same good manners that they do when greeting you.

Chasing

Dogs have an instinctive prey drive that can often lead them to bad habits such as chasing small animals like cats, squirrels, or even smaller dogs. If your puppy grows up with a cat, they will probably only chase them during play. However, dogs will often still have the urge to chase stray cats or other small animals when outside and they enjoy doing so. It is important that your dog is not encouraged to chase other animals as this could lead them out into the street if they are outside unleashed. While you cannot actually stop your dog from wanting to chase animals, you can prevent this behavior by going back to one of the first basic obedience commands you taught your dog or puppy, the "stay" command.

Make sure you first have your dog's focus in an inside and controlled environment, and continually practice "stay" over a period of time to be sure that your dog responds correctly to it. Once you are confident that your dog or puppy understands this command, you can take your dog outside on an extended lead and practice the stay command in your yard. To make this more challenging, you can take your dog to a closed but still exciting place (like a dog park) to practice this command. This will be an excellent opportunity to practice for a situation where your dog will want to chase because you can instruct your dog to "sit" and then "stay", essentially telling them that even with the other dogs and excitement, they need to remain focused on you. Unfortunately, you won't know if your dog will obey commands over their instinctive prey drive until it happens. However, by practicing the "sit" and "stay" commands in a variety of environment, you should be able to gain confidence that should your dog focus on a cat during your walks together, you can instruct them to "stay" and they will remain calm rather than trying to run off after their "prey".

YUCK! Rolling in "Dirt"

One very frustrating bad behavior that a lot of dogs have taken part in at some point in rolling in dirt, or worse. Most long-time dog owners would be able to tell you about a time that they let their dog out in the yard, park, or somewhere else and they rolled in dirt, garbage, an animal carcass, or a wild animal's droppings. For some reason some dogs seem to find joy in this disgusting act, but why do they do this? Why do dogs want to roll in something that stinks?

Some professional dog trainers think that it goes back to their ancestral instincts and that dogs roll in filth because wolves used to try to cover their scent with that of grass eating animals in order to elude their prey on hunts. Other dog training professionals say that it is just the opposite: and that dogs often roll in filth because they are trying to mark the "mess" with their scent. Regardless of why dogs roll in filth, it is not fun to have to bath your dog more often than necessary because they decide to roll. So how do you stop it from happening?

Unfortunately, there isn't a specific command that will teach your dog that he needs to override his natural instincts to roll in a mess. However, there are several ways that you can prevent this from becoming an issue. First, try to keep your yard free of feces (be it your dogs, stray cats, or wild animals) so that when you let your dog outside without a leash he will not have anything to roll and dirty himself in. Another thing you can do to prevent this habit is keeping your dog on a short leash when walking. This will prevent your dog from finding a mess before you get to it and he consequently won't have time to roll in anything undesirable.

Separation Anxiety: What Is It and How Do I Fix It?

Separation anxiety in dogs and puppies is a very common problem, however, the actions that your dog takes when feeling anxious can bring a lot of stress and frustration to you as his owner. Most owners of dogs who suffer from separation anxiety describe their dog's behavior as barking, scratching, whining, and destroying things around the home when the owners leave the house. In severe cases, the anxiety felt by the dog who has been left alone can lead their destructive habits to cause them to find a way out, and they can run frantically from the home once they have done so. Most owners who have dogs that suffer from separation anxiety will often crate their dogs when they have to leave the home, to prevent them from causing harm to themselves or damaging the home while their owners are away. However, sometimes crates prove ineffective as dogs who suffer from severe separation anxiety can sometimes bend the crate's bars or door in order to escape and be free to roam the home destructively in their owner's absence.

Getting rid of separation anxiety is different for every dog, as there is no one sure fire "cure all" that is guaranteed to solve the problems. Some dog owners are forced to turn to medication on their veterinarians to help their dogs remain calm and behaved when they have to be left alone, however, we have some tips to help you ease your dog of his anxiety before you feel you have to turn to medicating your dog to resolve the issue.

One of the best things you can do to help ease your dog's separation anxiety is to downplay it. Do not try to anticipate that there will be a problem before you leave the house, as your anticipation and anxiety will cause your dog to act out once you have left him alone. Try not to make a big event of leaving; take your dog to use the bathroom about fifteen minutes before you leave, calmly get ready to leave the home, and then ignore your dog as you go out for the day. This way the attention isn't on your dog, and he won't feel that "something is up" for him to act out upon destructively. Coming home should be much the same way as leaving your home, do not make a big event of it. Calmly come in the home, set your stuff down, and then calmly pet your dog or take him outside to relieve himself. The best way to ease your dog's separation anxiety is to show discourage any extra excitement that he would associate with you either going away from or returning to your home.

Another way you can help ease your puppy's separation anxiety is through exercise and training. Be sure to exercise your pup as much as you possibly can before you have to leave your home, this way he will not be feeling all that excess energy when he is left home alone. If you are able to talk your dog to a park or outside to play before you have to leave your home, he may feel tired and sleep for the majority of the period in which you are away from home. Training is also helpful in reducing destruction caused by separation anxiety. While you cannot directly train away separation anxiety, you can train your dog against the destructive behaviors he feels the need to act on every time you leave. By teaching your dog he is not allowed to shred, scratch, or chew on your things when you are home, he should follow his training and know that these negative behaviors are also off limits when he is left home alone.

If you do have a dog or puppy that seems to suffer from separation anxiety, be sure to give them an outlet to reroute their energy to after you have left the house. Make sure your dog or puppy has plenty of toys to chew on and play with while you are away, as these will keep his mind occupied and give him a release for that energy that is not your sofa or tennis shoes. You can also purchase toys that release treats as your dog plays with them at your local pet supply store. Things like chew toys and treat release toys take more time and are therefore better for your puppy to have to play with while home alone. Make sure to leave him a variety of toys while you are gone as well, as your puppy may become easily bored by the one or two you have left behind and go looking for trouble after the first hour alone.

One more way to help your dog's separation anxiety is by changing the way in which you get ready to leave the house. Humans are often creatures of habit, we like familiarity and often follow the same set of steps in the same order to get ready every day. Your dog will often pick up on these steps and will begin to associate simple actions (such as you putting on your shoes, locking the back door, or grabbing your coat) with you leaving the house. Try getting ready in a slightly different order each time, or put your shoes and jacket on thirty to sixty minutes before you are ready to leave the house so that your dog does not directly associate that with you leaving. You can also try leaving your purse and keys in a different location each time you come home (living room one day, then your bedroom, then the entryway) so that your dog does not have a set location with the things you take just before leaving him alone to focus on.

Not all dogs act upon their separation anxiety in the same way, so it is impossible to give just one way that will help ease the separation anxiety of all dogs. By following a few of these simple tricks you should be able to help your dog become less excited by you leaving the home (and also returning to it). Crate training can help dogs with separation anxiety, especially in the beginning so you can work on them being left out of the crate in small durations alone over an extended period of time. Again, some veterinarians will prescribe medication for your dog's separation anxiety and while this does calm their senses it does not actually cure the problem (and acts as a Band-Aid for the underlying issues present).

Chapter 7: Socializing Your Dog

Why Socialize My Puppy?

While socializing your puppy may not seem like an essential part of training, having your puppy willingly accept new dogs in a friendly manner will benefit you greatly in numerous situations. If your puppy or older dog is not socialized, you may have to worry about their behavior going from friendly to aggressive when you are out walking in your neighborhood, visiting friends or relatives who have dogs, or in public places where other dogs are present (such as stores, parks, or veterinarian's offices). Some groomers, kennels, and "doggy daycares" are less likely or will not accept dogs who have a tendency to be aggressive in any given situation (for the safety of the other animals present), so it will likely save you frustration later on down the road knowing that your dog will remain friendly in situations where he is introduced to other dogs.

How to Socialize My Puppy?

Socializing your puppy is an extremely simple concept, and it is important to begin doing so while your puppy is between eight and twelve weeks of age if possible. Before your puppy turns three months old, he is more accepting to new situations, experiences, and environments. This is why it is important to begin socializing your puppy early, while he is more accepting of new experiences and does not have a reason to fear. If you wait too long to begin socializing your puppy, he may begin to fear new dogs as he does not have any positive experiences with meeting them in the past. Waiting to socialize your puppy could make the process not only more challenging but also a lengthier process because of your puppy's fears or nervousness when introduced to new situations.

Begin socializing your puppy by taking him around other friendly dogs or puppies (where both dogs remain a leash for safety). This can be done during your neighborhood walks, at parks or recreational spaces, and at pet stores or other stores where dogs are welcome visitors. Do this several times, with new dogs each time if possible, to teach your dog that they will meet a variety of dogs and puppies while always associating these meetings with positive experiences. Be sure to encourage your puppy and praise him anytime he shows interest in the other dog.

When your puppy is a little older (between twelve and twenty weeks of age) and is comfortable meeting other dogs or puppies on a leash, you can try taking them to play in a more exciting environment like a dog park. It is important to show your puppy the other dogs through the park fence first if possible, as it can be overwhelming to have multiple unleashed dogs run to greet him at once after you have entered the park. If this is possible, allow your puppy to get as close to the fence as he would like at his own pace. Allowing your puppy to take his time to comfortably greet the other dogs will help him be much more relaxed once you take him into the fenced park to meet the other dogs without the fencing between them.

However, taking your dog or puppy to the dog park will allow your puppy to socialize with and meet other dogs while at the same time allowing him the space to run and play to release energy. Many dog parks have a rule that if a dog shows any sign of aggression they must leave immediately and not return, so you should not have to worry about your puppy's safety (always err on the side of caution just in case, however, most owners are respectful of this rule for obvious reasons). One thing to take notice of with dog parks is to make sure your puppy is on a preventative dewormer and has all of his or her vaccinations, as you can not prove that the other dogs present have all received responsible medical care and you would not want your puppy to get sick because of it.

Selecting a good dog park is also important for socializing your puppy. You want to take your puppy to a park that keeps clean water available for the dogs as stagnant water can house mosquitoes and other insects. It is also important to find a dog park where the owners take care to clean up after their dogs.

Conclusion

Thanks for making it through to the end of *Dog Training: A Guide to Your New Best Friend,* let's hope it was informative and able to provide you with all the tools you need to achieve your goals whatever they may be.

The ability to train your dog is one of the most important skills a dog owner must possess. Always remember that dogs should be treated with a lot of understanding and consideration. Dogs are intelligent, loyal, and if you train them properly, they can be the best pet anyone could have. Training your dog requires a lot of patience and this book aims to make the process a little easier.

The next step is to apply all the things you have learned from this book to have a fun and wonderful day-to-day experience with your new best friend.

Finally, if you found this book useful in any way, a review on Amazon is always appreciated!

Description

Have you recently adopted a dog and you are looking for a guide how to train him/her? Then, look no more! This book is specially written for people who are new to having a dog around.

Inside you will learn,

- The importance of training your dog
- Basic commands to teach your dog such as sit, shake, down, come, stay and leave it
- Tips on how to effectively house and crate train your dog
- Events and sports you can participate with your dog
- Tips on how to correct your dog's bad habits
- How to effectively ease your dog's separation anxiety
- Why is it important to socialize your dog
- **And so much more...**

Grab a copy of this book now and start your journey with your beloved dog!

Lightning Source UK Ltd.
Milton Keynes UK
UKHW02f2137061117
312302UK00007B/277/P

9 781975 968229